SMART© Marketing

The **FUN**damentals of Building and Expanding
a Successful Financial Advisory Practice

LARRY BIEDERMAN

DORRANCE
PUBLISHING CO
EST. 1920
PITTSBURGH, PENNSYLVANIA 15238

Dorrance Publishing Co
585 Alpha Drive
Pittsburgh, PA 15238
Visit our website at *www.dorrancebookstore.com*

ISBN: 978-1-4809-8898-9
eISBN: 978-1-4809-8852-1

Dedication

The marketing techniques detailed in this book are pertinent to both senior advisors who desire to expand their business and new Financial Advisors who are interested in improving their odds of success. Historically, less than 50% of new financial advisors last in the business beyond 24 months. The percentage is lower today for a number of reasons that we'll touch on later, but I'm confident that I would have been one of the casualties when I started with Merrill Lynch in 1965 had it not been for the guidance of the most successful broker in my Merrill Lynch office in Columbus, Ohio, Frederick "Fritz" Kahn.

Because of Fritz's invaluable advice, I succeeded beyond my wildest dreams and enjoyed a thirty-year career with the firm. While managing four offices and three regions of the Firm from 1972 to 1998, I developed the SMART©Marketing process to help others succeed and to repay the enormous debt I owe to Fritz. This book is dedicated to him.

Contents

Gets the advisor face to face with many qualified prospects
Innovative
Minimum of rejection
Using an enjoyable method
Definition of success: Face to face appointments with five new
    qualified prospects per week
When you know how to do it
When you don't know how to do it
    The Advice process
    Case study #7
    The power of asking for advice
    Asking clients
        Case study #8
        Case study #9
    Asking acquaintances
        Case study #10
    Asking strangers
        Case study #11
        Case study #12
What is no or poor advice?
Handling the "I already have a broker" objection
Obtaining personal introductions

Why meet prospects face to face
    Two goals of the Initial Appointment
        Build rapport and trust
        Gather business and personal information
    Location of the first meeting
        Your office
        Their home or office
    Why meet on their turf?
        They're more comfortable
        Learning about them
        Opportunity to include their spouse
        Their brokerage statements

1
Introduction

First, a little insight into the word play in the title of this book, "FUNdamentals." I grew up in Lima, Ohio and during the 1940's, spent a great deal of time with my grandfather, a retiree from the Lima City Fire Department. He had taken early retirement due to a disabling injury and supplemented his pension by babysitting for my brother and me while our parents worked. He had experienced a difficult life - the Great Depression, his injury, and my grandmother's chronic ill health. Despite this, he was an enthusiastic, positive and optimistic person. I'm not sure how many times he offered me this career advice but it really stuck. He said, "Larry, I don't care what you choose to do in life but make sure it enables you to do two things. One, make a lot of money! As I read later, "having a lot of money won't guarantee happiness, but it will allow you to enjoy your misery in some nice places."

Second, make sure whatever career you choose will allow you the opportunity to have a lot of fun. He didn't mean just lighthearted fun - he meant it in a deeper sense: enjoyment, fulfillment, satisfaction, the joy of accomplishment. He said "when you get to be my age (70's), I don't want you to look back and wish you would have done things differently. Whatever you do, make sure you make a lot of money and have a lot of fun."

My grandfather's advice became my philosophy throughout my Merrill Lynch career. The advisors in the offices and regions I led will confirm that our motto was always "to make a lot of money and have a lot of fun." My main goal in writing this book is to show you that building or expanding your business doesn't have to be painful. It can be fun, hence the title "The FUNdamentals of........."

My first jobs after graduating from Ohio State in 1959 afforded little of either money or fun. I had absolutely no idea what I wanted to do after leaving school, but I did know one thing – that with a wife and our first child on the way I had to start making a living.

From June, 1959 to June, 1965 I changed jobs often hoping to find an ideal career. During that period, I was a tennis club professional, a life insurance salesman, a bank management trainee, an Eastman Kodak photo products salesman, and a first-year law student. I found none of these fulfilling and was at wit's end when a fraternity brother who was with Merrill Lynch suggested that I interview for a job in the Columbus, Ohio office as a broker, or account executive, as we were called in those days at Merrill. The office manager there was a huge photography buff and based mainly on my 3 years of sales experience with Kodak, he hired me on the spot at an impressive salary of $450 a month, less than half of what I had earned at Kodak before resigning to attend law school.

My father, whose impression of stockbrokers was formed during the Great Depression and who had never owned a stock or bond, went beserk when I told him that I was quitting law school to become a broker. He said, "you don't have any money; you don't come from money; you don't know anyone with money; you know nothing about stocks, you hated selling life insurance, and now you're going to be a stockbroker. You'll never make it! You should crawl back to Rochester and beg Kodak for your job back."

However, I knew that I "HAD" to make it. I was 27 years old with a wife, two children, a twelve year old Chevy, and $35 in the bank. If you've been there yourself, you know the feeling.

In those days, we had to successfully complete Merrill Lynch's six month training program before being allowed to sell stocks and bonds – three months working and studying in your branch office and three months of classroom training in the company's New York headquarters. I had so little money that I had to borrow $500 from my father-in-law to make the New York trip.

Desperate to succeed, I studied hard and paid attention in the classroom. The highlights of the program were weekly talks from some of the most highly productive brokers in the firm who shared their success stories with us. Since they were Merrill Lynch legends, I listened closely to each one and took copious notes. Knowing that my manager was going to ask me how I was going to build my business when I got back to Columbus and having learned a lot about marketing at Eastman Kodak, I built my own prospecting plan from the ideas of Merrill's best brokers.

Sure enough, on day one back in Columbus, the manager called me into his office and said, "Ok kid, how are you going to build your business?" I confidently handed him a copy of my five page prospecting plan and started to describe my ideas. After about thirty seconds, he threw my plan in the waste basket and said, "did they teach you this stuff in New York? If the folks in the Training Department knew how to make it, they wouldn't be in the Training Department. They would be out here making it! Do you want to know how to make it in Columbus, Ohio, kid? See that telephone, see that telephone book? You get on the phone and make 100 cold calls a day and you'll do just fine. Now get to work!"

Since he was the boss, I took his advice and started cold calling prospects. I called during the day from 9 to 5 and four nights a week from 7 to 9PM. I had excellent prospect lists since my mother was a legal secretary and showed me how to get information on who was buying and selling houses, commercial real estate, businesses, expensive cars, boats, and even airplanes. I had no problem identifying money in motion, but couldn't get anyone to talk to me, a complete stranger, on the phone. Some people were polite and said no nicely. Most were not so polite and hung up rudely, screaming "never call me again!"

After a few weeks of this, I had opened just one account - a recently widowed, lonely, older woman. She welcomed my calls, so I called her almost every evening and discovered that she had $700 to invest. My manager had suggested that General Motors was a good buy at $100 per share so I sold her 7 shares of General Motors at $101. That year, 1966, the seventeen year bull market peaked and General Motors topped out around $100. It headed steeply lower, ending the year in the 50's and ten years later, was selling in the 20's. So, after several weeks as a broker, I had one client with $700 rapidly heading south. I wasn't making any money and certainly wasn't having any fun. My father took great pleasure in rubbing it in. "How's it going son?" "How do you like being a stockbroker?" "I told you so!"

The most successful broker in Merrill Lynch's Columbus office at that time was my respected friend, Fritz Kahn. Fritz produced over $300,000 in commissions per year at a time when $100,000 was the recognized level of excellence in the industry. He was a great guy and had been very helpful to me as a new trainee. I went to Fritz, told him that I was having a very difficult time, and he said, "let's go to lunch, rookie." After I told him about my cold calling experiences and total lack of progress, his first words were, "who are you trying to call on?" When I told him "anyone," his statement was that if you try to do business with anyone, that's just what you'll get – anyone.

Fritz suggested, "instead of calling on anyone, why don't you call only on people that you know have money to invest?" And, instead of calling on everyone, why don't you specialize and call on only three types of prospects; people in no more than three "target" markets?" He advised me to become an expert in dealing with wealthy clients in just three target markets. That day at lunch he asked me to tell him the three target markets in which I intended to specialize.

Off the top of head, I told him that I would target three types of prospects: physicians in my home town of Lima, aerospace engineers at North American Aviation, one of the largest employers in Columbus, and since one of the speakers at our training class in New York had mentioned that pilots made great clients, I said that my third target market was going to be officers at Lockbourne air force base in Columbus, the largest SAC base in the world.

We finished lunch, Fritz said "go to work," and my results started turning up in just two weeks. I finished the year in the top 5% of Merrill Lynch first year brokers. Although I didn't realize it until twenty years later, the first step in SMARTMarketing (Selecting) was created at lunch with Fritz. More on "Selecting" in chapter three.

2

Failure in the Financial Services Industry

I mentioned earlier that prior to the mid-to-late 90's, the failure rate of advisors/brokers in their first two years had historically been around 50%. As Merrill Lynch's Director of Sales and Management Development in the mid 1970's, I had access to firm and industry statistics on the issue. For years, the traditional hiring and training approach in the brokerage business was to hire as many candidates as possible, throw them up against the wall, and see who sticks. The profitability structure of the business prior to May Day, 1975, allowed for this approach.

In fact, I knew managers at Merrill Lynch and other firms who claimed that since no one could predict success, hiring new advisors had to be a "numbers game," just like prospecting. "The more you hire and weed out, the better your chances of getting a few to stick." Some of these managers were recognized by their firms as successful leaders who others were urged to emulate. I often heard them boast about the number of new brokers they hired and fired.

This approach seemed to me to be a complete waste of financial and human resources - a huge failure of leadership, and I resolved, as a new manager in 1972, to do a better job. However, the success rate of the approximately twenty rookies I hired from 1972-75 in my first office management assignments in Chicago and New York City was the same as the industry average. After two years, only 50% of the brokers were still in the business.

In hindsight, it was easy to identify some of the failures as hiring mistakes, good people who did not have the work ethic or aptitudes to be successful brokers. It was obvious that I had to do a better job of hiring. But other individuals, who were not hiring mistakes, also failed despite our best efforts to train them. Even though we provided our young brokers with the most advanced sales training of the era, such as the Xerox Selling Skills Program, we were able to improve only slightly on the traditional 50% industry failure rate in the two offices and two regions I led from 1977 to 1986.

In 1989, after twenty-four years of brokering and managing, I retired from Merrill Lynch to start my own consulting firm, Biederman and Associates. Our mission was to help financial services professionals (advisors and managers) make more money and have more fun in their professional lives. We decided that the most important contribution we could make would be to solve the rookie turnover/productivity issue and went to work full-time on the problem and its causes.

One day, the light bulb came on. I thought that if a manager had a good stream of qualified applicants, was using proven techniques to hire only those best qualified, but was still getting only average retention results, the problem had to lie in training. How were rookie advisors being trained to build their business?

We found that aside from vastly improved product, service, financial planning, and technology training, there had been little innovation in marketing training for years. New advisors were still being told by trainers and managers that prospecting was a "numbers game" and that if they just made enough cold calls, they would be successful. Remember, the recommended number of calls in 1966 was 100 dials per day. By 2000, that number was up to 300-400 dials per day at Lehman Bros., the best known cold calling firm in the country.

Lehman's approach was necessary since they had only a few offices in the country. They couldn't possibly reach prospects across the country face to face. The other fact about Lehman's cold calling program was that it made sense from a cost effectiveness standpoint. In the 1960's they hired out of work actors on a part time basis to make cold screening calls for $5 an hour. If they managed to find a live prospect, they turned the call over to an experienced producer who went on to try to close the deal.

Contrast this with the major national firms who had hundreds of branch offices around the country. Instead of paying $5 an hour, they hired college graduates (many with advanced degrees) or experienced business people at $40M to $100M salaries plus substantial benefits. They located them in some of the most prestigious, expensive office space in each city, and then taught them to make cold calls, open accounts, and close the business by themselves – a far different and more expensive approach than Lehman's given the wash out rate of 50-90% of these rookie brokers.

In the 1990's, a few consultants and trainers, recognizing the increasing futility of telephone cold calling due to customer resistance, the 100+ million people on the National Do Not Call list, and technological barriers like Caller ID and Call Blocking changed the rules of the numbers game. Instead of hundreds of phone calls, they advocated mailing thousands of direct mail pieces each month or sending thousands of email messages. I realized that nothing had changed – marketing/prospecting in the 1990's was still regarded as a numbers game. The problem was that most affluent people, don't want or need to be a "number" and unlike the 60's, 70's, and 80's, they had alternatives to cold-calling brokers.

To solve the problem, I decided to go "back to the future." I reread my 1965 training school notes from the most successful Merrill Lynch brokers in the 1960's. I thought about how Charley Merrill built the most successful retail brokerage firm in the 1930"s, in the very heart of the depression when people detested stockbrokers. I remembered Fritz Kahn's advice in 1966. I reflected on my own prospecting successes and failures. I read Tom Stanley's very successful book, "Marketing to the Affluent" and attended several of his lectures. I also reflected on conversations with literally hundreds of successful Merrill Lynch brokers I had met over twenty years with the Firm – very few of whom had built their business by cold calling.

In 1990, based on this research I developed a seminar program labeled "Back to the Future" until a very bright young female broker in Texas, attending one of the seminars, said afterwards, "aren't you talking about working smarter rather than harder? Then, why don't you call your program SMART©Marketing?"

By 1993 I was giving SMART©Marketing seminars to hundreds of new advisors across the country and receiving tremendous feedback of marketing success stories. Early that year I received a call from Tom Muller, an old friend. Tom was the Director of Merrill Lynch's Western Sales Division. One of his

Districts, Southern California, had problems. It consistently had the lowest productivity, the highest turnover, and it was 30th out of 30 Merrill Lynch Districts in its rookie success rate.

Over the years in Merrill Lynch management meetings, I had heard the Southern California managers rationalize their low productivity and high turnover. They blamed it mainly on:

1. Advisor work ethic: Since Southern California advisors had a "surfing mentality," they just didn't work as hard as those in other parts of the country.

2. California weather reinforces the poor work ethic. The managers said that "if our weather was like Detroit, Chicago, or New York, our advisors would spend more time in the office."

3. They felt that the high turnover was due to the fact that advisors in Southern California tended to be disloyal and moved from firm to firm more often than their peers around the country.

4. Southern California was a "conspicuous consumption" society. Appearances were very important there and people tended to spend more and save less than clients in other parts of the country. They therefore had less to invest.

5. Besides, if they do have money to invest, they prefer real estate over stocks and bonds.

6. And finally, the Pacific time zone is a definite barrier to high productivity since the market opens at 6AM and is closed by 1PM. Our clients just don't have as much time in the day to do business as those in the other time zones.

It wasn't difficult to dismiss these reasons as pure rationalizations. The facts were that competitive firms in Southern California were out producing Merrill Lynch. They had more advisors and less turnover. Given the enormous wealth in the area, Merrill was significantly under-brokered. The market could easily support at least double the number of Merrill Lynch advisors, but no one had been able to grow the sales force given the traditional turnover rate. Improvement in Southern California would have an enormous impact on the results of Tom's Division. He asked if I would be interested in coming out of retirement to lead the Southern California District.

I knew that SMART©Marketing techniques had worked in the 60's, 70's, and 80's, but despite the positive feedback from the attendees of my 1990-93 seminars, I wasn't 100% sure that they were applicable to the current environment in Southern California, however I couldn't resist the challenge. Southern California seemed to be the perfect place to test my concepts and as the District Director, I would have the positional authority to initiate, reinforce, and instill SMART©Marketing in the ranks. I told Tom that I would take the job if allowed to implement my own hiring and training techniques. He had enough confidence in me to agree and the rest is recorded Merrill Lynch history. From 1993 to 1998:

- Market share in the District increased from 24% to 30% while Merrill Lynch's national market share was declining from 31% to 27%

- Since turnover fell drastically, we were able to grow the salesforce from 475 to over 900 advisors in five years.

- The District led the firm in new advisor success rates in 1996 and 1997 at 85%

- Southern California rookies averaged significantly higher production than their Merrill Lynch peers in year one through three:

Advisor Average Production per Year

	So. Cal.	ML
Year 1:	$68,000	$41,000
2:	$179,000	$109,000
3:	$315,000	$225,000

Our experienced advisors also grew their production at 125% of the firm average during those years. We trained them in the same SMART©Marketing techniques as our rookies.

Southern California advisors had the same products, services, and technological support as the rest of the firm and most of our competitors, the same economy and stock and bond markets, and the same compliance regulations. There had to be a reason for the productivity differentiation and I believe that the reason was SMART©Marketing.

I retired for the second time from Merrill Lynch in 1998 and helped found PSBtraining.com. Eventually, our clients consisted of virtually all national, regional, and large independent financial services firms. By that time the turnover problem of young brokers, or Financial Advisors as most were now known, had become a real epidemic in the industry. Instead of the 50% failure rate, some firms were experiencing 80-90% losses and the profitability structure that had previously supported the "throw 'em against the wall" approach no longer existed. Discount brokers, internet investing, and increased competition from banks, insurance companies, and fee-based financial planners led to reduced spreads and lower commissions. Now it was financial suicide to continue to hire and train large numbers of rookies. Some firms dropped their training programs, others cut back on hiring, and many professionals were quoted as saying "rookies just can't make it in the business today."

Executives, branch managers, and trainers rationalized the higher failure rates as:

1. More competition
2. More informed and sophisticated clients with almost unlimited investment options and pricing
3. More complicated products and services
4. Technical innovations like caller ID, call screening, call blocking.
5. The National Do Not Call list
6. Poor work habits of the GenXers

But my partners and I knew the real reasons – hiring and training. Just as I had experienced in 1989 - 92 with Biederman and Associates and in the Southern

California District from 1993-98, good hiring and the right marketing training would produce quality results. Therefore, our lead product at PSBtraining.com in 1999 became SMART©Marketing. We taught it to thousands of advisors across the country.

As with most new ideas, many firms, managers, and advisors didn't accept the non-traditional concepts of SMART©Marketing, preferring instead to stick to the old cold calling methods. However, one regional firm in the southeast enthusiastically adopted the new marketing techniques and over the next few years, starting in the poor market environment of 2002, completely reversed their rookie results, improving from a success rate of approximately 20% to over 70% and moving from dead last among seventeen regional firms to the top quintile. Consequently, over the next five years they were able to improve average advisor productivity from $229M to over $450M and grow their sales force from 700 to 1100 with resultant contributions to firm profitability.

If the Southern California District and a regional firm in the southeast were able to improve their productivity results with SMART©Marketing, I'm sure that you can too!

3

The Necessity for a New Approach to Marketing

As we discussed in the previous chapter, the traditional approach to prospecting/marketing in the industry was that "it's a numbers game." New advisors were taught that if they had the fortitude to make thousands of cold calls and could tolerate rejection rates of well over 90%, he or she could "make it" in the business. Even in the best of times – the tremendous eighteen year bull market in stocks and bonds beginning in 1982, this approach led to a rookie success rate of no more than 50%.

It also led to an average production in the industry of approximately $300,000. The 50% who made it through the first two years took three more years to reach the $300,000 level and then they hit a production plateau. It appeared that they were willing to tolerate the pain of prospecting until their income approached $100,000, then they just quit business building. At some firms like Merrill Lynch the plateau was higher ($400M-$500M) and at many smaller firms, lower ($200M-$300M), but the plateau effect has been a reality in the industry for years.

The bust of the dot.com boom in 2000 sent a shudder through the industry. By 2003, the rookie failure rate at many firms was approaching 70-90% and a few very smart people in the business had begun talking about the need for a new approach to prospecting. As early as 1996, John Bowen, President of CEG Worldwide, wrote "according to a new study by "The Institutional Investor" most wealthy clients prefer to meet financial advisors through a friend or acquaintance." In 2002, he followed with an article "The Best of Times" in which he stated "to be successful in today's market, you must focus on relationship based marketing."

That was the first time I became aware of any consultant to the industry, other than Tom Stanley or myself, advocating that prospecting/marketing was not a numbers game. It was, as SMART©Marketing had been teaching, a relationship-based activity. By 2010, the cat was out of the bag. That year in "What Your Wealthy Clients are Thinking," a research study by the Oechsli Institute and Investment News, Matt Oechsli published the following about affluent clients:

1. "They don't like salespeople and are skeptical of marketing campaigns."

2. "Only 2% are influenced by cold calling."

3. "Only 6% are influenced by public seminars"

4. "83% said they had a negative feeling when asked for a referral"

5. "Don't send me any more brochures."

6. "I'm not bringing friends to an event."

The study concluded "that the marketing tactics of yesterday will not work today." In his follow up research the next year Oechsli wrote that "many affluent clients stated that they would meet with an advisor **"ONLY THROUGH A PERSONAL INTRODUCTION FROM A TRUSTED FRIEND, FAMILY MEMBER, COLLEAGUE, OR ANOTHER PROFESSIONAL"** and he ranked the most effective marketing tactics of 2011 from best to worst as follows:

1. Introductions
2. Strategic networking
3. Referral alliances with CPA's, attorneys, etc.
4. Unsolicited referrals
5. Solicited referrals
6. Intimate client events
7. Seminars
8. Direct mail
9. Cold calling

Tragically many trainers, managers, and veteran mentors are still telling rookies that cold calling is the only way to make it in the business. I vehemently disagree with that assertion.

SMART©Marketing is the essence of relationship based marketing and assuming that

a. new financial advisors have the intelligence to pass the industry's rigorous registration examinations
b. they fit the aptitude profile of successful advisors
c. they have the necessary work ethic, and
d. they receive the product and service training and support that the typical firm provides, there are only five skills that they need to master to be inordinately successful in their first few years and none of them is cold calling. They must be able to:
   1. Identify affluent prospects
   2. Meet them face to face
   3. Build rapport (trust and affection) with these prospects
   4. Earn their business with superior business and personal service
   5. Leverage their best client, prospect, and center of influence relationships into many others.

These five skills are the essence of SMART©Marketing:

1. Selecting – identifying affluent prospects
2. Marketing – getting face to face with them
3. Affiliating – building rapport with them
4. Responding – earning their business with superior business and personal service
5. Triggering – leveraging relationships

Now, let's get into the details of SMART©Marketing.

4
Selecting

The first step in becoming a SMARTMarketer is Selecting, identifying affluent prospects or, in our terms, targeting prospects from two or three "niche or natural" markets." Instead of blindly calling on anyone and everyone, we suggest that you focus on becoming a specialist or expert in reaching no more than three types of potential clients.

In 1997 the VIP Forum conducted two studies for its member firms: "Client Prospecting and Retention in the High Net Worth Market" and "The Newly Wealthy – Cultivating and Serving Wealthy Clients." The Forum followed in 1999 with "The Newly Wealthy; Best strategies for Targeting the Entrepreneur and other Beneficiaries of Sudden Wealth.

In those studies, three marketing methods were often cited as particularly effective:

1. Niche Specialization
2. Networking in the niche
3. Referrals from the niche

In other words, the studies confirmed what Fritz Kahn had known thirty years earlier!

Tiburon Strategic Advisors, in its 2005 report, "Consumer Wealth, Target Markets and Strategies," stated that "the competitive playing field for advisors is getting crowded…. and that "will compel advisors to develop strategies for specific target markets."

As we stated earlier John Bowen of CEG Worldwide wrote in 2005 that "…. …. you must focus on relationship-based marketing by developing a target market and discovering niche opportunities."

Registered Representative magazine also published an article in 2003 stating that "brokers who create a niche practice earn upwards of 50% more than generalists because:

1. They understand their clients better.
2. Prospecting becomes more efficient due to "word of mouth" advertising by clients in the niche.
3. In-depth relationships lead to greater wallet share.

Niche marketing is powerful for three primary reasons:

1. Marketing: by specializing in specific types of clients, you can become an expert in reaching prospects in your niche.

2. Planning and investing: You can become an expert in the financial needs of people in your niche and the products and services to meet those needs.

3. Leveraging: People in the niche tend to know and talk to each other and because of your reputation with them, when they talk about investing, they often talk about you. You have the most effective type of promotion at work for you, word of mouth advertising.

Case study #1:
One young advisor from the aforementioned southeastern regional firm took advantage of these three reasons to become a huge success. PF was age 26 when he attended my first SMART©Marketing seminar sponsored by his firm in 2002. He had been registered for fourteen months and had commission revenue of only $25,000 in that time. He told me that he certainly wasn't making any money nor having any fun and was ready to quit the business. After attending the seminar, PF became an instant SMART©Marketing success.

Niche specialization: He decided to focus on one niche, blue collar retirees from the leading electric utility company in his state. He chose the blue collar employees because he looked much younger than his age and as a rookie, felt that he would have trouble relating to the senior executives of the company.

Marketing: utilizing the "Advice Process," a technique that we will introduce in the next chapter, he learned how to efficiently and effectively meet his prospects. He attended their Quarter Century Club dinners in the twelve company locations around the state. He put 50,000 miles on his car that year driving to the dinners.

Planning and investing: He found that his prospects were approximately the same age, 60-65. They all had about the amount in their 401(k), $300-400,000, and most had the same investment needs – income and preservation of capital. Consequently he offered these clients the most conservative and highest quality mutual funds and annuities that his firm offered.

Leveraging: Since PF became well known among the employees of the company, when they talked about retiring and rolling over their 401(k's), they talked about him. Consequently, his business grew geometrically. The year after attending our seminar, he produced $300,000 and the next year, became the firm's youngest President's Club member with over $500,000 of production. Two years later he was producing over $1,000,000, still focused on that one niche. Because he did such a great job with his clients, the company asked if he could handle their retirees in two adjoining states.

Characteristics of a High Potential Niche

1. Affluence: People in the niche have a lot of money. They either have high incomes, are the beneficiaries of a wealth creation event such as a 401(k) rollover, or have accumulated wealth over their lifetimes via savings.
2. Quantity: There are a lot of affluent people in the niche.
3. Affinity group: People in the niche know each other because they all work in the same company, industry, or profession; or they all live in the same community; or they all belong to the same club or enjoy the same sports or hobbies. It's essential for effective word of mouth advertising that they know each other.
4. Point of entry: It's ideal if you already have a good relationship with someone in the niche. If so, you will have a leg up in obtaining introductions to your prospects. However, this is not essential. If you're

smart and motivated, you can find a way to meet people in your niche. I knew no one in any of my first three niches, but I was so hungry to succeed that I found points of entry into each.

5. Enjoy: You have reason to believe that you like and can relate to people in the niche. If you want to have a lot of fun in your business, you have to do business with people you like. If you like them, chances are it will be easy to build relationships with your prospects and they will like you. It's a fact that people like to do business with people like themselves.

Types of niches:

PF's story has been replicated by SMART©Marketing advisors across the country. Some focus on business and professional niches: orthodontists, physicians of Asian descent, Southern California dairy farmers, Proctor and Gamble retirees in Tennessee, Verizon retirees in Tampa, Florida, UPS managers in the midwest, office supply industry executives, entertainment industry producers, directors, actors, actresses, and studio executives, biomedical industry executives, professional athletes, etc.

Some specialize in their ethnic niches: Greek, Vietnamese, native American, and Chinese. In Southern California there are many wealthy Chinese Americans. We established an office in a predominantly Chinese-American community and staffed it with advisors who spoke Chinese. The office was almost immediately profitable. Visiting the office was fascinating, listening to our advisors speak to their clients in Cantonese and Mandarin.

We also found that there was a very significant Vietnamese community in Southern California. In fact, there was an area known as little Saigon. However, we had few if any Vietnamese clients. As you might expect, the reason was that we had no Vietnamese advisors. Hiring several of Vietnamese ancestry in 1994, our business in the community immediately soared.

One young man of native American ancestry focused on casino executives around the country since many casinos were owned by Indian tribes.

As my psychologist friend, Dr. Loretta Malandro, says: "whether we like it or not, it's a fact that people like to do business with people like them." If you want to do business in a particular ethnic niche, it's a huge advantage to be of that ethnic background.

Other advisors focus on geographic niches: wealthy retirement communities, gated country club communities, neighborhoods, towns, cities, suburban, and rural areas.

A person's work experience prior to becoming a financial advisor may also be a great niche. If there's affluence in that occupation or profession, don't overlook or dismiss it as a great potential natural market. You probably know the business well and have relationships in the field, but many new advisors are reluctant to approach people with whom they've worked in the past. They fear they will not be credible as a financial advisor because they've been known as a printer, trucker, CPA, health care worker, etc. That concern is more in the mind of the advisor than that of their contacts in the field. I've known many advisors who have become almost instantly successful because of their knowledge and contacts in their prior field.

Case study # 2
One of our new hires in Southern California was a great example. When I arrived there in 1993 it seemed odd to me that Merrill Lynch had only one Hollywood celebrity as a client. I was told that the reason was because the celebrities were shielded by their agents, making them almost impossible to reach. We ran an employment ad in "Variety," and hired an ex business agent as a financial advisor. He knew virtually every accomplished agent in the industry and many of their clients. Consequently, in his first week of production, he opened accounts with two celebrity clients with over $40 million in assets and went on to become a top producer with our firm. Hollywood was his natural market.

Case study # 3:
Another of our hires, the wife of one of our most successful advisors, had been working in the venture capital health care field for a number of years when we met. She knew many of the industry executives on a first name basis and had

been featured on the cover of "California Health Care," one of the most prominent publications in the industry. I suggested that her potential as a financial advisor was unlimited and convinced her to join us.

She was an instant success, producing over $500,000 in her second year. She was also the only retail advisor I've ever known who our investment bankers called for advice and introductions.

Case study # 4:

A third example of a pure rookie successfully building his business in his prior field was John, a young man who had worked in his family's trucking business for twelve years. He asked me how he should get started and I suggested that he use the Advice Process (next Chapter) with the Director of the California Trucking Association whom he knew. She suggested that he make a presentation at their next quarterly meeting and told him that the most pressing financial need many trucking company owners was what to do with their business when they retired. If their children did not want the business, what were their options?

He had been an advisor for only one month and obviously didn't know anything about business divestitures, so we introduced him to an expert in our New York headquarters. That person came out to California to make the presentation. The results were amazing. Eight trucking company CEO's requested appointments with John. He opened three 401 (k) plans, and received invitations to address regional and national trucking company meetings on the same topic. His practice was jump started because he went back to the field he knew to begin his advisory career.

Other fortunate advisors have built their practices with people who share their passion in life, their hobby or sport such as private aviators, deep sea fishing enthusiasts, yacht and marina owners, wealthy tennis players, amateur and professional golfers, cutting horse owners, antique car collectors, etc.

Case study # 5:

One young financial advisor who joined our Newport Beach office in Southern California from a competitor firm, was rumored to be the "cold-calling" king of his former branch. He had been only moderately successful there, as he was working hard but not "SMART." After joining us, he attended our SMART©Marketing training and we discovered that his passion was deep sea fishing, a niche with tremendous potential as the Newport Beach harbor is filled with multi-million dollar, privately-owned fishing boats.

Starting to build relationships within the niche, he volunteered for the Hoag Hospital charity fishing tournament. Within two years of focusing on his new niche, he had tripled his business and by his own admission, was making more money and having more fun in the business than he had ever dreamed. He has since gone on to become a multi-million dollar producer with fishing enthusiasts and several years ago brought in one of the largest retail accounts ($3.5 billion) in Merrill Lynch history from a contact in one of the international fishing conservation groups.

Talk about having fun! How would you like to build your business with people who love to do what you love? We know that people like to do business with others like them. If you have a passion in life and people of affluence share your passion, you probably have a high potential niche at your fingertips.

Case study # 6
A rookie advisor from a major national firm attended one of my SMART©Marketing seminars in Atlanta. Typically, he told me that he was having a very difficult time establishing an affluent clientele by cold calling, the method his firm almost exclusively advocated. He said he had a degree from Embry Riddle Aeronautical University and had been a flight instructor in Atlanta before coming into our business. He said that he no longer flew as he was too busy working, ie cold calling. I suggested that he was overlooking his ideal niche market since most of the people he had trained were affluent and they obviously trusted him. He took the advice and resumed flight instructing on weekends. Within a few years he was one of his firm's largest producers in Atlanta.

Today he still focuses almost exclusively on private aviation and has narrowed his niche to Cirrus aircraft owners. A few years ago he called to tell me that his practice was growing so rapidly that he was going to have to add another advisor onto his team. Cleverly, he hired a former Cirrus salesman as his new partner.

Characteristics of a high potential niche:

There are five basic characteristics of a high potential niche:

1. People in the niche are affluent either through high average income or a wealth creation event such as a sale of business, 401(k) rollover, or inheritance.

2. There are a large number of potential clients in the niche, employees, professionals, owners, etc.

3. They belong to some kind of an affinity group: company, industry, trade association, club, community or geographic area. In other words, they know and interact with each other which generates the most effective kind of advertising, word of mouth.

4. Ideally, you have a point of entry into the niche, a client, center of influence, friend or family member. This is not essential as an enterprising advisor can usually find a point of entry, but it can expedite the process.

5. You already know or think that you can relate well to people in the niche – you like them and they like you. If you want to have fun in your practice, it's essential that you do business with clients you enjoy.

How many niches should you focus on?

We recommend that an advisor focus on at least three niches for three primary reasons:

1. One may be impossible to penetrate
2. One may not be enjoyable
3. One may disappear

Penetration
One niche may be difficult to penetrate because a competitor has a dominate position in the niche for pricing, service, or other reasons. For example, one

24

young advisor in the Southeast was planning on specializing on 401(k) rollover prospects with one of the largest corporate employers in his state. He thought it would be a great niche because there were hundreds of retirees from the company annually with significant 401(k) rollovers. But he found that the company allowed their employees to work only with three pre-approved firms who were providers of the firm's 401(k) plan. He and his firm were effectively precluded from the business.

Another advisor in the Northeast planned on focusing on pilots of one major airline with a hub in his city – on the surface a great niche for him since his best friend was a pilot with the airline. However, his friend advised him that when the pilots reached fifty, their company provided them with a free $5,000 financial plan from one of the top-rated planning firms in the country. The pilots were very satisfied with the firm and he would have a very difficult time competing with their advisors. He decided on another niche.

Enjoyment

If your career goal is to have a lot of fun in your job, you'll find that it's essential to do business with people you enjoy. I mentioned earlier that I originally thought a good niche for me would be the aerospace engineers at North American Aviation in Columbus. They were highly paid and there were hundreds of them at the North American facility just a few miles from my Merrill Lynch office. I had no problem reaching them by conducting investing classes at the plant, however I found very quickly that I did not enjoy dealing with engineers. They were all nice people but were extremely detail oriented and wanted reams of research information before taking any kind of action. They were also laboriously slow decision makers. After opening two accounts with engineers, I moved on to another niche, wealthy tennis enthusiasts in Ohio, who shared my interest in the sport, were easy for me to reach and establish rapport with, and were generally folks I enjoyed much more.

Another FA in the south had built a good practice with supervisors at the petroleum refineries in his area. He asked me if he had been mistaken by not focusing on the senior executives of the companies. He had grown up in a blue collar family and enjoyed dealing with blue collar folks up to the supervisory level, but was clearly uncomfortable talking with executives. Since he enjoyed his supervisory clients and they had six and seven figure accounts which allowed him to produce almost a million dollars a year, I suggested that he continue to focus on the people he enjoyed and forget about the executive suites.

Disappearance

I mentioned earlier that one of my first three niches was pilots at Lockbourne Air Force base in Columbus. It actually became my favorite niche. I enjoyed the officers and their spouses immensely. They were great people, risk takers, decision makers, and excellent savers with strong interest in investing. Furthermore, the cocktails at the Officers Club were only 25 cents – how good does it get! Had Lockbourne been my only niche, however, my practice would have suffered when the Air Force decided to close the base not too many years later.

So, for these reasons, we strongly recommend focusing on at least several niches. More than one offers diversification and protection and two or three are not too many to prevent you from becoming a specialist in your niches versus the generalists you'll find as your competitors.

Finding your niche

Remember, the first step in becoming a successful SMART©Marketer, is to identify the type of affluent people you want as your clients, to identify your potential niches. As Cuba Gooding so memorably said in the film, "Jerry McGuire," "SHOW ME THE MONEY!"

So where's the money. Well the first place you can start to identify your niches is with your present clients, prospects, contacts, or centers of influence. Since you already know these folks, do any of them fit the criteria for a high potential niche,

Action Steps:

1. Assess yourself – your educational and employment background, personality, interests, and hobbies. Are there affluent people who share

your traits? If so you may have a "natural market" like one of mine. I had been a ranked tennis player in the juniors, played number one singles and doubles on my high school and college teams, and had been a teaching professional briefly after college. I was actively playing amateur tournaments in Ohio during my early years with Merrill Lynch, knew the top amateurs in the state, and played frequently in invitational tournaments at their clubs. Therefore, it was very easy for me to relate to these players and their fellow members of the top tennis and country clubs in Ohio. It was a "natural" market for me, one of my three niches throughout my producing career.

Case study # 7

One of my favorite examples of someone discovering his "natural market" is an advisor with the southeastern firm I mentioned earlier. Fred was 65 years old when he attended one of my SMART©Marketing seminars for senior producers. Before the program, he explained that he was not there to learn how to expand his practice. In fact, after some twenty years in the securities industry, he had topped out at the $400,000 level. He was bored, tired, and wanted to quit so that he could devote full time to his real passions, rodeo bull riding and his ranch in Colorado. He said he was only attending the seminar because he had heard that I had years of experience in the industry and he hoped I could tell him the best way to "sell his practice" and retire.

I said we could chat about selling his practice after the seminar but since he was already there, perhaps there was a way to enjoy the ranch, take advantage of his interest in bull riding, and, at the same time, substantially increase his production and income. After the section of the program on Niche Specialization, the thought dawned on Fred that professional bull riders fit the description of a high potential niche.

Fast forward several years, Fred was 70 years "young" and more excited than ever about his advisory practice. His production was now over $1,000,000 annually. He was spending 50% of his time at his ranch and weekends attending rodeos. One of his clients was a legend in the bull riding profession who cofounded the PBR (Professional

Bull Riders Circuit) and helped Fred expand his business with a number of professional bull riders. The last time I saw Fred, he was excited about extending his marketing efforts beyond the riders to the breeders of rodeo bulls. He told me that he was definitely making more money and having more fun than any time in his advisory career.

If you don't have a natural market, you should ask yourself "where is the wealth creation in my marketing area?" Is there a particular industry or certain types of businesses, one or more professions, a geographic area such as a wealthy suburb, retirement community, or exclusive gated communities. You must be able to identify and relate to affluence to be successful as a financial advisor. I call it "smelling the money." I'm often asked "how does one smell the money" and my response is that I'm not sure but if you can't do it, don't come into our business.

Once you've identified your natural and/or niche markets, you must now determine how to get face to face with prospects in your markets. You've got to become a marketing expert in your niches. Marketing is the second step or the "M" in SMART©Marketing.

5
Marketing

My definition of marketing probably wouldn't fly at the major business schools, but for the purpose of SMART©Marketing and being successful as a new financial advisor or growing your practice as a senior producer, it's very simple: getting face to face with qualified prospects. It's the second step to success in your first year but as many failed advisors discovered, it's easier said than done. The failure to successfully market or prospect is undoubtedly the number one reason for the historically high failure rate among rookie brokers and it's also the reason why many brokers who survive the first few years inevitably plateau in production and earnings after their early years. They simply don't want to continue prospecting because they perceive it as painful and most human beings avoid pain at all costs.

The pain results from the incredibly high rate of rejection stemming from cold calling, or "smiling and dialing" with the product of the day, week, or month as it's known in the business. Unfortunately, it has always been and remains to this day to be the standard marketing method of most firms in the industry. It results in a rejection rate that can easily approach 100% and few advisors can deal with that much rejection. Unfortunately, no one (trainers or managers) has taught them how to minimize rejection with other approaches.

You may remember that my manager in 1966 pointed me toward the telephone and the Columbus phone book and said, "if you want to make it in this office kid, you'll get on that phone and make 100 calls a day. You'll open one new account a day and you'll do just fine." I mentioned the meager results of that method in chapter one, but fortunately, with Fritz's help and some luck, I found a better way.

In SMART©Marketing we teach that the objectives of marketing are:

1. To get the advisor face to face with affluent prospects

2. Using an innovative approach
3. With a minimum of rejection
4. Using a method that they enjoy. Yes, enjoy!

Because, if your marketing method works and you enjoy it, you'll keep doing it. If you keep doing it, you'll make more money and have more fun. Sound familiar?

So the objective is to find an innovative method of marketing in your niche, to differentiate yourself from the "cold call cowboys" of your competition. Sometimes you already know how to do it based on your knowledge of the niche. For example, I mentioned that one of my niches was affluent tennis players in Ohio. I knew instinctively how to meet them – by playing in invitational tennis tournaments at their clubs.

There was a summer circuit of weekend invitational tournaments held at the best tennis and country clubs around the state: Dayton, Cincinnati, Columbus, Toledo, Cleveland, Mansfield, etc. The formats were usually the same – a draw of 32 ranked players with the first round on Friday afternoon. That evening there was the inevitable cocktail party and dinner. Attending were those of us playing in the tournament and members of the club and their spouses. It was very easy to meet and talk with the members that evening.

On Saturday there were two more rounds followed by another party Saturday evening, usually more formal. It was a second great opportunity to meet and build rapport with more members of the club and their spouses at cocktails and dinner.

On Sunday, the semis and finals were played, offering one more chance to spend the day with the club members. It was then very easy on Monday to call these folks and ask for the opportunity to "earn a portion of their investment business." The call was what is known in the business as a "warm call" and the rejection rate was nearly non-existent. At the worst I heard "I already have a broker or I'm already taken care of." I don't consider either of these a rejection, but rather as an indication of interest and my challenge then became taking the client away from a competitor, something that often wasn't too difficult to do.

SMART©Marketers around the country have found innovative and enjoyable methods of getting face to face with prospects in their niches, such as:

- attending cutting horse competitions
- volunteering at charity deep sea fishing tournaments, steeplechase events, and polo matches.
- Flight instructing in one's spare time. Don't try it unless you're a qualified pilot.
- Sponsoring free golf clinics for doctors and other professionals who love golf
- Joint sponsorship of investing clinics with luxury automobile dealers and exclusive jewelers,
- Gourmet cooking clinics in Viking kitchen showrooms
- Wine tastings in the wine cellars of exclusive restaurants
- Fly fishing and hunting equipment demonstrations with top outdoor retailers
- Teaching investment classes and other speaking engagements
- Media: radio, TV, magazine, newspapers, and trade publications
- Civic and charitable participations
- Forming network groups of professionals in other lines of work, ie life and casualty insurance, CPA's, attorneys, residential and commercial realtors, builders and architects, party and wedding planners, etc. One very successful advisor in the southwest has kept her networking group together for twenty years. They meet every Tuesday morning for breakfast with the purpose of learning more about each other's business and sharing referrals. These referrals have helped her to produce over $3 million annually and consistently rank among the largest producers in her national firm.

As we stated earlier, too many people in the industry believe that there's only one way of marketing, ie cold calling. In his excellent book "Boot Camp for Financial Advisors," David Clemenko states that there are nine ways. Although David is obviously more enlightened than the hidebound cold calling traditionalists, I must respectfully disagree with his thesis.

There are an infinite number of ways to build your business In devising innovative marketing activities, you are limited only by your own creativity, the knowledge of those whose advice you've sought, and by your firm's legal and compliance restrictions. Obviously, anything you do has to meet legal, ethical, and professional standards, but given these natural limitations, the world is your oyster. Remember, please don't believe it when someone tells you that there's only one or nine ways to make it in this business.

Assuming that you don't know how to get face to face with affluent people in your niche, there's a fool proof way to discover the right method. In SMART©Marketing, it's known as the "advice process." I stumbled upon it within a few days of attempting to market to physicians. After telling Fritz at lunch that my first niche was going to be doctors in my hometown, I went back to the office, got out the Lima yellow pages and started calling doctors' offices. It only took an hour or two to realize that getting through the receptionists was hopeless.

So that evening I tried calling them at home and found that not only was it unproductive, it was an exercise in futility and masochism. I was called a number of unprintable names that evening by the doctors whose evenings I had disturbed.

Since cold calling obviously didn't work with doctors, I tried direct mail. Merrill Lynch had just published a new booklet and eye-catching mailer on attractive growth stocks. My wife and I hand addressed one hundred mailers to the doctors in Lima. A few days later I received one coupon back and I recognized the name, a very successful radiologist whose daughters had been a year behind me in high school. I had even attended a summer party at their very expansive home.

Since I smelled money, I decided that rather than mailing the book and calling a few days later, I would deliver it to Dr. E in person. I drove 90 miles to Lima, pulled up in front of his office building, and there on the ground floor was the major brokerage firm in town, Thompson McKinnon. What luck – I thought, should I make the call or go to a movie? Since I had only one client with seven shares of General Motors rapidly heading south, I decided to make the call.

I walked into the office, gave the receptionist my card and told her that Doctor E had requested the book. I asked if I might hand it to him. She said, "have a seat."

It was a typical doctor's waiting room, ten chairs with patients waiting for their appointments and reading magazines. It soon became obvious that I was going to be there for at least a couple of hours as about every fifteen minutes Dr. E would come out of his private office and warmly call the name of the next patient.

Finally, it was my turn. "Biederman," he rather harshly announced and I walked across the room expecting him to invite me into the private office. However, Dr. E's body language did not appear promising. He was frowning, standing stiffly with crossed arms and holding my business card. As I approached him, he posed four questions in an accusatory fashion: "your name's Biederman?" "You're with Merrill Lynch in Columbus? "You're a stockbroker? "What the hell are you doing here?"

By now the other patients had put down their magazines because the little docudrama they were witnessing was a lot more interesting. They were about to see me get my a—handed to me.

I responded, "Dr. E, you requested this book on growth stocks. I thought I would bring it to you and ask for the opportunity to earn a portion of your investment business." If the last twelve words of the sentence sound familiar, they should because they're the same I used with every new prospect.

The words were taught to my New York training class in 1966 by the number one broker at Merrill Lynch, David Stahlberg. David said that anyone who wouldn't give you the opportunity to "earn" a portion of their business, was a jerk and rather than them rejecting you, you should reject them!" Since I've always thought that copying genius was better than inventing mediocrity, I never varied from David's script. He was a genius!

After asking Dr. E for the opportunity to earn a portion of his business, I shut up. A few seconds (which seemed like hours) later, he said, "young fellow, I've been doing business with those bastards downstairs for twenty years and no one has ever walked upstairs to see me. How much business would you like to earn?"

We went into his office and thirty minutes later I walked out with my first 1,000 share order on which the commission was $450 versus $17.95 on the seven shares of GM. That night I was wide awake at 3AM, staring at the ceiling, and thinking: "Dear God, this is the kind of business I want to do. I want to write 1000 share orders for doctors in Lima. I've tried calling and I've tried mailing, but have only one client to show for it. What should I do?"

My prayers were answered with the Advice Process – where the idea to ask for Dr. E's advice came from, I'll never know, but as they say in golf, my favorite sport, some times it's better to be lucky than good.

The next morning I used the advice process for the first time. I called Dr. E to tell him what he had paid for his stock and asked, "Doctor, do you have a few minutes to give me some advice?" He said "sure, what can I do for you?"

"I said "I would like to build my practice with other successful doctors in Lima. Do you think that would be a good idea?"

He said that it would be an excellent idea because my only competition was the "bastards downstairs" so I asked, "if you were me, how would you do it?"

He thought for a minute and then said, "How often can you come to Lima?" I told him at least once a week and he said, "I want you to meet me in the St. Ritas hospital cafeteria on Wednesdays at noon. The doctors don't have office hours or play golf on Wednesdays afternoons. They usually stay in the hospital and clean up their paperwork. That means most of them have lunch in the cafeteria. There's a round table with twelve chairs in the cafeteria. You meet me at noon. We'll sit at that table and any doctor who walks up that you don't know, I'll say, "oh doctor, have you met Larry Biederman yet? He's our broker at Merrill Lynch."

The first doctor who approached the table on the first Wednesday was Dr. H, the most successful orthopedic surgeon in Lima. Dr. E introduced me as promised and Dr. H said "so you're a stockbroker. What do you like?" I responded "I don't know." Dr. H said "what kind of stockbroker doesn't know what he likes?" I answered, "Dr. H, what I like for Dr. E, I might not like for you. It depends on what you're trying to do with your investments. I would have to sit down and chat with you about that. Taken aback, Dr. H asked "do you come up here often?" I told him that I came to the hospital every Wednesday and he said, "let's have lunch next week." Think about how long it would have taken to have lunch with the leading orthopedic surgeon in town by cold calling?

(In Chapter 6, Affiliating, I will expand on why I answered Dr. H's question in this manner. I will also cover my recommended answer to the other stereotypical question stockbrokers are often asked, "how's the market." Both questions are usually good naturedly intended to get the stockbroker talking, a communications trap that most advisors are too often more than willing to fall into.)

The next week Dr. H and I had lunch at a table for two in the corner of the cafeteria. He handed me a manila envelope full of stock certificates. I asked "what is this?" Dr. H said "Dr. E says you're going to handle our investments, are you or aren't you? If you are, take this mess and tell me what to do with it!"

There was over $1,000,000 worth of securities in the envelope and Dr. H had become my largest client after only a few minutes of chatting with him at lunch the week before. Why? I'm convinced that he and many other doctors at the hospital became my clients because of the introduction from their trusted colleague, Dr. E.

Earlier I cited a 1996 article in "Financial Planning" magazine by John Bowen of CEG Worldwide. Mr. Bowen quoted a 1996 "Institutional Investor" research study that indicated "most wealthy investors prefer to meet a financial advisor through a trusted friend, acquaintance, or organization." To me the study confirmed that the secret to successful marketing/prospecting is leveraging established relationships and the "Advice process" is a powerful tool in generating that leverage.

Thirty years later I was conducting a SMART©Marketing training program for some senior advisors in the Southern California District. Dr. Charles Dwyer, a world renowned professor from the University of Pennsylvania and an expert in the principles of human influence, was one of our speakers.

He heard me explain the "advice process" in class and later asked me if I knew why asking for advice is so effective. I said that I knew it worked but didn't understand why. He told me "asking for someone's advice is one of the most powerful things you can do to positively influence that person and that once they offer their advice, they become committed to it success."

Thinking back to Dr. E at St. Ritas hospital, I realized that not only did he tell me exactly how to favorably get face to face with other doctors in Lima, he became my de facto marketing agent in the medical community in town - he was committed to seeing his advice, and me, become successful.

Case study # 8

Over the years, I've enjoyed hearing success stories from many SMART©Marketers who've successfully used the advice process. One of our Los Angeles producers, Jeff, was an experienced FA with over $750,000 per year in commissions. Since his goal was to reach the $1,000,000 level, he tried the advice process with one of his best clients, the CEO of a major Los Angeles corporation. He told him that he would like to expand his practice with other executives in the client's industry. Did he think that would be a good idea and if so, how should he do it.

The client indicated that he was chairman of the industry's annual charitable fundraising effort and he thought it would be a good idea if Jeff attended their kickoff dinner in New York where he would introduce him to other CEO's in the industry. In fact, he continued, "perhaps you and your wife would like to fly to New York on the corporate jet and spend the weekend in our corporate suite at the Waldorf Astoria with my wife and me." How's that for having fun!

One year later Jeff had over fifty executives in the industry as clients and had exceeded his $1,000,000 goal. The client became a marketing agent for Jeff in his industry because of the advice process.

Case study # 9

Another advisor in our District, Ron, had been stuck at the $400,000 production level for several years. He tried the advice process with his best client, a Georgia orthodontist. Over the phone, he asked the client if he thought it would be a good idea to expand his practice with other successful orthodontists and if so, how should he do it. The client told Ron that it was a good idea and suggested a great method for meeting other orthodontists. Once a quarter the client conducted three-day training sessions in new orthodontia techniques and usually 5-10 orthodontists came to his office to participate. The client's advice was that Ron attend the sessions. He would meet and spend three days with the group and on the last day of the session, the client would tell the other doctors how well Ron had done for him, and invite Ron to describe his investment process.

Ron's production soared over the next few years from $400,000 to the $2,000,000 level and the only difference in his practice was that instead of having one orthodontist as a client, he had over sixty.

Case study # 10
One of the top Financial Advisors in New York City attended one of my SMART©Marketing seminars but was very skeptical of the Advice process. On the lunch break he told me that he was going to phone his best client and try it. He said if it didn't work, after lunch he would tell the class I was full of s—-! My only request was that he use the advice script word for word.

He called his best client, an owner of five McDonalds franchises. He asked if the client thought it would be a good idea to expand his practice with other owners of multiple McDonalds franchises. The client said yes and the FA said, "if you were me, how would you do it?" The client responded that he and some of his peers met for dinner once a month in the city. He suggested that the FA attend one of the dinners as his guest and he would introduce him to all of his McDonald's friends. The FA came back into the classroom after lunch and told the other attendees, "this s—- really works!"

In each of the instances we've discussed so far, the advisor asked a client for advice. It is not necessary, however, that the person be a client. We have recorded success stories where advisors have asked a family friend, a prospect, an acquaintance, even a perfect stranger for advice and gotten the same response.

Acquaintance:
Case study # 10
Kalid, of Pakistani descent, was an experienced producer in Los Angeles stuck at the $300,000 production level, the typical production plateau in the industry. At a SMART©Marketing seminar, he told me that he had the perfect person

to ask for advice – an acquaintance also of Pakistani ancestry who had just sold his company for over $100,000,000 and was highly respected in the California Pakistani community. Kalid said that he was afraid to ask the man for his advice and asked if I would be willing to do it. I thought it would be a great experience.

We invited him for lunch at my club and he brought his CPA, as he obviously thought we were going to try to sell him something. After a delightful lunch where we talked about how he had built his company, his personal background, and, of course, Pakistan, I asked him if he had a few minutes to give us some advice. I said that Kalid would like to expand his practice with other successful people of Pakistani heritage, did he think it would be a good idea, and if he were Kalid, how would he do it.

The man and his CPA conversed in Urdu for several minutes then he turned to us and said; "there are many successful Pakistani businessmen and professionals in Southern California, but they don't know much about the American capital markets because it is against our religion to lend or borrow money at interest. We suggest that Kalid offer investment classes. Since Pakistani life centers around the mosque, we think that is where he should hold the classes and we'll help him arrange them.

The next year Kalid's production grew from his normal $300,000 to over $1,000,000 from attendees at his classes. The wealthy businessman and his CPA made sure that their advice was successful. How would you like to have a $100,000,000 success helping promote your practice?

A Perfect Stranger
Case study # 11
I mentioned earlier that one of my first, and most enjoyable niches, was the officers at Lockbourne Air Force Base in Columbus. This was during the Viet Nam war and no one just walked onto a Strategic Air Command base – there were sentries with guns and dogs at the gates. Most officers lived on the base and there was no telephone directory available to the general public. I had no idea how to get face to face with the pilots and other officers.

One day I called the base public affairs office and told them that I was interested in expanding my investment practice with officers at the base. The person told me that she didn't know anything about investing, but perhaps I should speak with the base Financial Officer, Colonel G. She transferred my call and a few seconds later, I was talking to the Colonel, a perfect stranger.

I introduced myself and asked if he had a few minutes to give me some advice. He said sure and I started through the advice script:

> Me: "I would like to build my investment practice with officers at Lockbourne. Do you think that would be a good idea?"
>
> Colonel G: "Many of the officers at the base have an interest in investing so it would probably be a good idea."
>
> Me: "If you were me, how would you go about becoming known at the base?"
>
> Colonel G: "I think it would be a good idea to offer investment classes at the base. Could you teach an investment class out here?
>
> Me: Sure. "Merrill Lynch has a four-session class on How to Invest and I would love to teach it at Lockbourne. What would be a good way to advertise the classes?"
>
> Colonel G: Why don't you run an ad in the base newspaper and see what kind of response you get"

I arranged for the ad and two weeks later, I had received fifty positive responses. The first night, there were fifty attendees in the auditorium at the officers' club, but not one pilot – it was their wives. Each night after the lecture as I was putting my notes away, a little line would form at the podium – wives who would ask if they and their husband, when he got back from the Med or from Viet Nam, could come to my office and talk to me about investing. After the four classes, I had over twenty clients at Lockbourne, all thanks to the advice of a perfect stranger, Colonel G.

Case study # 12

Joe, a rookie advisor in Southern California, was a Mormon. I suggested that wealthy Mormons would probably would be a good niche for him. However, he had grown up in Utah, had only lived in Southern California a short time after graduating from college, and didn't know any affluent Mormons in Orange County.

I asked him if he knew "of" any very successful Mormons. He indicated that one member of his congregation, an attorney, was purported to be the largest tither to the church each year, but Joe had never met him. I suggested that Joe call him, introduce himself as a member of the church, say that he was just starting his business career with Merrill Lynch in Orange County, and ask for a few minutes of his time for some advice.

Joe called and the lawyer immediately suggested that Joe come to his office where they could talk. After a few minutes Joe started into the advice process. The attorney cut him short with "Joe, are you looking to meet Mormons with money?

Why don't you have breakfast with me and one of my clients on Saturday." Joe did and was introduced to a woman who had just sold her hotel across the street from Disneyland for $200,000,000. Unfortunately, she decided to work with a more experienced team of advisors from another firm, never-the-less, Joe produced over $250,000 in his first year with Merrill Lynch, most of his clients resulting from introductions from the attorney who became his marketing agent in the Mormon community.

Since we've worked with so many advisors who have tried the advice process, we know that it doesn't always result in a workable marketing plan. Sometimes, the person you're asking for advice says, "I don't know how you would market to others like me." At that point, you can quit or you can take the process one step further by saying: "I understand that but let me ask you just one more question. Besides yourself, who are the three or four most successful people in your company, industry, club, neighborhood, etc – whatever the niche you're trying to penetrate.

In the first stage of the process, you asked an open-ended question, "if you were me, how would you do it?" Now you're asking a closed-end question, "who are the three or four.........?" The person will always know three or four others in their niche.

After they've mentioned their names, ask the following, "should I be calling on them?" Quite often the answer will be no because "I'm sure they're already taken care of" or "I'm sure they already have a broker." You'll hear these lines many times in your career and you must have a response because statistically, everyone already has a broker. In fact, if the client has $1,000,000 invested, research indicates that they probably have at least three advisors.

You may devise a more clever response, but the aforementioned David Stahlberg, the number one Merrill Lynch producer in the 1960's and 70's, taught me the following:

Response to an existing client: "Remember when we met, you had another broker? Just like you, all of my best clients already had a broker before we met, but they found that my team and I provide a level of service that the other broker can't match." In light of that, don't you think I should be calling on them?"

Response to a non-client: "All of my best clients already had a broker when we met but we found that they usually had one or more of the following problems:

1. They were taking more risk than necessary.
2. They were paying too much in fees or commissions.
3. Their investments were underperforming.
4. They were receiving very poor service.
    I would really like to explain this to _____. Don't you think I should be calling on them?

If the answer is still no, move on. You've probably hit a stone wall. However, if the answer is yes, then ask "if you were me, what would be the best way to contact them?" There are several very positive things that can happen after that. The person might just pick up the phone and call them for you. I had that happen several times, once was an introduction to the wealthiest person in my hometown which I will describe in the chapter on Triggering.

The person might say "I'll be happy to introduce you" or "why don't you just phone them and tell them I told you to call?" If they don't offer to make an introduction, they might say, "I don't know. How do you normally contact a new client?"

At that point, you should say, "new clients prefer to meet me through an introduction from a trusted friend. Would you be willing to introduce me or send this letter (item # 1 in examples) for me?" (always have a copy of the introductory letter with you.)

Case study # 13
Josh was just starting out as a new financial advisor in Westchester County, New York. He asked a physician friend of his parents for his advice about building his practice with successful physicians there. The doctor agreed to send a letter recommending Josh to 175 doctors in his referral network. The advisor followed up with phone calls and got appointments with 130 of the prospects. Why did the doctors agree to see him? Because, he was introduced by a trusted associate.

The SMART©Marketing Advice Script

The advice process is based on the principle that asking someone for their advice is one of the most powerful things you can do to positively influence that person and once they offer their advice, they become committed to its success. The objective of the advice process is to obtain a marketing approach that will get you in front of potential clients just like the person whose advice you are soliciting.

Script

FA: Mr./Mrs/Dr._____, do you have a few minutes to give me some advice?
- It's important to ask this because the person will be flattered that you value their advice and let them know immediately that you are not asking for an order.

Client/Prospect/Center of Influence: Sure

FA: I would like to expand my practice with other (_____) just like you. (Important: be very specific in describing who you're looking for. Do not under any circumstances, say "other successful people like you." They will not understand who you want.) **Do you think that would be a good idea?**

FA: If the answer is no ask **"Oh, why not?" The reason may be valid or, more likely, it will be: "I'm sure they're already taken care of" or "I'm sure they already have an advisor." The response to this objection is covered in # 4 below.**

At this point, the person may:
1. Give you some excellent advice about marketing to others like themselves in which case you will want to implement it immediately.
2. Give you some ineffective advice, ie
   a. "Get a list of other (_____) and just give them a call." Now you've got nothing better than a cold call list which probably won't work. Suggest to the person that most people today don't appreciate cold calls; that new clients today prefer to meet an advisor through an introduction from someone they know and trust and ask if the person would feel comfortable introducing you to two or three others in the niche.
   b. Rent a booth at our annual convention next year." The person may be well meaning but this is marginal advice at best. First the convention is usually too far into the future and, second, unless you have something really unusual to offer, you'll find it hard to make any serious contacts at the booth. However, thank them for the advice and say that you will look into it but in the meantime,

"besides yourself, who are the two or three most successful (———
———) that you know?"

3. Say something like "let me think about it." If this is the case, make sure you follow up with the person in no less than a week to get their thoughts. If they still don't have an idea, proceed to the "besides yourself" followup question in points 2 and 4.

4. Tell you that they have no idea how you would do it. At this point, you can say: **"I can understand that but let me ask you one more question, who are the two or three most successful (_____) that you know.** Once they give you the names, ask: **"Should I be calling on them?"**

    a. If the answer is yes: **"What would be the best way to reach them."**

        • The person may say something like, "how do you normally try to reach new clients"?

        • You say, **"new clients prefer to meet me through an introduction from someone they know and trust."** Would you feel comfortable introducing me or sending this letter?"

            ○ Dear _____, I'm writing to introduce my friend, _____. He is a financial advisor with (firm) and has been especially helpful to me in planning for our retirement. I'm sure he can do the same for you. He'll be calling in a few days to arrange a no-cost, no-obligation appointment. I'll take it as a personal favor if you would agree to meet with him.

            ○ As we mentioned above, the usual answer will be something like "I'm sure they are already taken care of" or "I'm sure they already have an advisor." To which your response should be: **"all of my best clients already had a stockbroker/advisor when we met, however they found that my firm and I can provide a level of service that their present broker cannot match.**

            ○ Another response might be: **"all of my best clients already had a broker when we met, but we found that they had one or more of these four problems:**

                • **They were taking more risk than necessary**

- **Their investments were underperforming**
- **They were paying too much in fees or commissions**
- **They were receiving very poor service**
- The bottom line is that at best you may come away with a creative marketing idea that will allow you to reach others in the niche. At worst, you may come away with two or three new prospects you did not have before the interview.

Many FA's have had spectacular success with the advice process. I hope you will experience the same. Good luck.

PS: A word to the wise: be sure to practice the script many times so that the questions and responses will flow naturally from your lips. The smoother you are, the greater your chances of success.

Sample introductory letters:

1. Letter from a current client:

Dear Sam,

I'm writing to introduce my (Firm) financial advisor and good friend, ………….. He's helped tremendously with my retirement planning and I'm sure he can do the same for you. It will be well worth your time t spend a few minutes with him. He'll be calling in a few days to request a personal appointment.

2. Letter from a non-client:

Dear Sam,

I'm writing to introduce my friend (………). She's a financial advisor with (Firm), here in the city. I think it would be well worth your time to spend a few minutes with her. She'll be calling in a few days to request a personal appointment.

3. Letter from you:

Dear Mr. Jones,

Our mutual friend, (.........) suggested that I contact you. Our team at (Firm) specializes in helping successful (niche) develop solutions to retirement planning and other wealth management issues. I would sincerely appreciate the opportunity to meet with you to determine if we might be of service. I'll call in a few days to request an appointment that will not obligate you in any way.

In all candor, these letters are the weakest form of personal introduction. Don't be surprised if the recipient doesn't even remember receiving the letter. However, the letters are certainly preferable to a telephone cold call.

Action steps:

1. Ask yourself if you already have a good idea for getting face to face with qualified prospects in your natural or niche markets. If so, put it into action immediately. You'll discover in a very short time if it is effective. If not, don't beat your head against the wall, find another method.

2. Memorize the Advice Script line by line so that it just rolls off of your tongue.

3. Use the advice process with someone who knows the niche: a family member, friend, acquaintance, center of influence, or anyone you think really understands the niche. Remember, you're not looking for a referral or a list of prospects. You want an innovative marketing plan that will generate favorable introductions to prospects in your niche. It's like the biblical parable: "If you give someone a fish, you feed them for a day. Teach them how to fish and you'll feed them for a lifetime." The advice for a marketing plan is teaching you how to fish.

Now that you've discovered how to favorably meet qualified prospects in your niche(s) using a method that you enjoy, it remains to simply "Do It!" If you do, the next step will be to establish rapport (trust and affection) in the first business appointment. We call this Affiliating.

6
Affiliating

Whatever marketing method you've employed to meet a potential client, there comes a time when you need to start talking business. In the past, this was often done on the first phone conversation or a followup call and the advisor and client might never meet personally. We strongly recommend in the current environment of distrust that you meet with your prospects face to face. Why?

The general public has grown increasingly mistrustful of Wall Street in light of the dotcom disaster in 2000, the 2008- 2009 market collapse, and the negative publicity generated by the Madoff and Alan Stanford scams. A report by the Securities Industry Association indicated in 2003 that 43% of investors surveyed said that distrust was the # 1 issue facing the securities industry, up from 8% in 2001 and the 2008 financial meltdown has undoubtedly served to increase that number. In fact, Wall Street in general and financial advisors in particular have probably not been held in such low esteem since the Great Depression of the 1930's.

But there's a lesson to be learned from that period. Charles Merrill founded the modern Merrill Lynch firm near the bottom of the depression in 1934 and ten years later, he had the number one retail brokerage firm. His strategy coined the famous phrase "Wall Street to Main Street" and he carried out that strategy by establishing offices all across the country. He did it so Merrill Lynch advisors could see their clients face to face because he knew that the best way to build trust was eye ball to eye ball.

In his book "The Power of Presence," Douglas McKenna says "when you need to connect at the deepest, most engaging level and when you need to build a bond of trust and understanding, there's nothing like face to face." Charley Merrill knew this instinctively years before.

There's an old saying: "those who forget the past are doomed to repeat it." Most brokerage firms have forgotten Charley Merrill's strategy. They've advocated telephone cold calling almost exclusively as a more efficient method of marketing. In my experience, the most efficient approach may not be the most effective.

I was taught by my first boss at Eastman Kodak, that faced with tough competition, you have two choices. You can either do what they're doing better or you can do something else. Since a cold call is a cold call and it's difficult to do it better than your competition, I believe strongly that if you want to differentiate yourself today, meet your prospects face to face whenever possible.

We call this face to face meeting the initial appointment. Although it's sometimes possible to open an account and get an order on the first appointment, this will happen only infrequently. Therefore, if your goal is to open an account on the first appointment, you will probably be unsuccessful and frustrated. A more realistic goal for the meeting is to build rapport (trust and affection) and to gather business and personal information, the more the better.

We recommend that you go to the client's home or office for the first meeting. Most advisors, for convenience purposes, want the client to come to them. One senior advisor at a national firm emphatically stated to me that he wanted the prospect to come to his office so they would see a picture of his wife and children. My response was that they didn't care much about his family but they really cared about their own!

A meeting on the prospect's turf is often much more effective. First of all, they tend to be more comfortable, open, and candid there. Secondly, you can learn a great deal about them just by noticing their pictures, plaques, and collectibles. In his bestseller, "Swim With the Sharks Without Being Eaten Alive," Harvey Mackay wrote that the most important reading a salesperson will do is the wall of his client's home or office.

Calling on a male prospect at his home is also a great opportunity to include the spouse, who quite often will be the decision maker or at least have a great influence in an investment decision.

Recent research indicated that only 12% of female spouses had ever met their husband's advisor and only 8% trusted that person. Think about this for a moment – given the actuarial tables, which of the spouses will probably end up with the investments? Establishing trust and rapport with the female spouses of your male clients, just makes good business sense.

Lastly, from a purely practical standpoint, most clients keep their brokerage statements at their home or office, not in your office!

Where ever you meet the prospect for the first time, it's important to understand a powerful rule of human interaction – the first impression. Dr. David Lieberman refers to it in his book, "Get Anyone to do Anything." He writes "our first impression of another person is crucial because everything we see and hear later gets filtered through that initial opinion."

In his best seller, "Blink," Malcolm Gladwell labels the process "thin slicing, filtering the few factors that matter" and says that we make snap judgments about others in as little as two seconds to two minutes.

Another psychologist, my good friend, Dr. Loretta Malandro, says that people decide if they like you in the first four to six minutes. She states that it's a purely subjective decision, made subconsciously and later validated with logic. She calls the interpersonal phenomenon, the "Eureka Factor."

She says if you want to use the Eureka Factor to your advantage, you need to know that people want to be fully understood and are most easily influenced by people they perceive as similar to themselves. Therefore, the most powerful communication skills you need in the first appointment are questioning and listening, not talking. Many financial advisors, both new and experienced, are inclined to do just the opposite. They want to talk about themselves, their firm, financial planning, or the market. Being inherently defensive about their lack of experience, young advisors in particular seek to portray themselves as professional by telling prospects how much they know. Unfortunately, they're doing exactly the opposite of making a good first impression.

They may also fall into a trap by answering one or, even worse, both of the two questions most brokers are stereotypically asked by someone they meet for the first time: "what do you like?" or "how's the market?" You may remember from my introduction to Dr. H in the hospital cafeteria that he asked me "what do you like."

Dave Stahlberg, who I've mentioned several times previously, gave us a great way to avoid this invitation to talk rather than listen.

When asked "what do you like," David would respond with "I don't know." Just as it did with Dr. H, this answer will more often than not evoke the response, "what do you mean you don't know? What kind of stockbroker are you if you don't even know what you like?"

David would then say, "what I like for one client may not be what I like for another. It depends on what they're trying to do with their investments. I would have to sit down and chat with you about what you're trying to do."

By the way, David advised us to always use the word, "chat" because it's warm and non-threatening. I've probably used the word thousands of time in my career with prospects, clients, advisors, friends, etc.

If asked the second question, "how's the market," David would say "I really don't care." This answer would usually induce the person to say something like, "what kind of stockbroker doesn't care about the market?" and he would respond with "what I've found is that in an up market, some stocks are going down and in a down market some stocks are going up. It depends on what you're trying to do with your investments. I would have to sit down and chat with you about that. In this way, David avoided the temptation to be the person doing the talking. He also put the ball right back into the other person's court and pointed the conversation toward the ultimate goal of having a serious conversation about the prospects' investment goals.

Even if many young advisors do understand the need to ask questions and listen, they tend to mistakenly start a conversation with financial questions. Many are trained to actually begin a meeting with a potential client on page one of the firm's financial planning questionnaire. We respectfully suggest that this is a good way to put the prospect's feet to sleep. Why not ask them about what they're most interested in, themselves?

There are two topics that most people love to talk about: the story of their success and their very strong interests or passions in life. In his book "Marketing to the Affluent," Tom Stanley writes that "when the affluent are allowed to tell the story of their success they often develop affection for the listener and affection has a great deal to do with success in selling."

Case study # 14

As an example, two young financial advisors wanted to develop a niche market in the entertainment industry in Los Angeles. Through an acquaintance they arranged a breakfast meeting with a very successful television producer. Approaching the table, the producer shook their hands and said "I'm really busy today, what can I do for you guys?" They responded that they would like to ask his advice but first, could he tell them how he had become so successful in television? He talked for forty-five minutes about how he had become the producer of one of the most popular television series of its time and then said, "you know, I really like you fellows. Tell you what I'm going to do, I'm going to bring you $100 million in assets!" By the time they related the story, via his introductions they had opened accounts with actors, directors, producers, and television executives with assets totaling over $60 million. They said at that point their biggest issue was to get him thinking bigger than $100 million.

We've heard many similar success stories from advisors who asked a prospect to share the story of their success. Why does it work so well? Just think how often someone gets to tell the story. Their spouses are tired of hearing it and their kids don't give a hoot.

Case study # 15

A very senior, successful advisor (Charley) in Texas attended one of my SMART©Marketing seminars in the early 90's. He was respectful in the classroom but his body language and lack of participation indicated that he really didn't want to be there. As I described the Eureka Factor, I asked for a volunteer to share with the class something that had happened to them in the last year that really impacted their life.

At that point, Charley volunteered to tell the class about his first granddaughter who had been born a few months earlier. As he spoke, his eyes lit up, he had a big smile on his face, and his gestures further indicated his love and enthusiasm for his new baby granddaughter, his daughter, and her husband. As he talked Charley was the perfect example of the power of the Eureka Factor.

I mentioned in the seminar that if anyone tried any of the techniques we discussed, please let me know. Two weeks later, Charley called and said, "I didn't want to attend your seminar, but you really impressed me with that Eureka Factor idea. I decided to try it with a prospect when I met him for the first time at his company, a credit collection agency. Credit collection businesses don't always have the best of reputations and I really didn't expect much but was amazed find a beautiful new building and an office filled with well dressed young people on the phones. The place was a bee hive of activity and obviously the company was very successful.

I finally got in to see the prospect and he said, "Charley, I appreciate your coming to see me, but I'm just swamped today. You have five minutes to tell me what you've got!"

Charley said that in light of the time constraint, he normally would have gotten right down to business by suggesting a stock or bond investment, but he remembered his Eureka Factor experience and said instead, "you've certainly have a great business here. How did you get started."

The prospect talked for almost an hour then said, "Charley, I've enjoyed our conversation but I am really busy." He reached into his desk drawer and pulled out two brokerage statements. "Why don't you take these accounts, get them transferred over, and tell me what to do with them?" The two accounts totaled $1,500,000 and Charley had not said one word other than asking about the man's success.

Case study # 16:

I had a similar experience with the owner of a tool and die business in Ohio. I was driving back to Columbus from Lima on Route 33, a highway that I had traveled hundreds of times. Just south of Bellefontaine, Ohio I spotted a building that I had never seen before, just a half mile or so down a side road. I pulled off the highway and drove to the building, a beautiful new one-story brick building. In the rear parking lot, there were thirty or so cars and in the front, two late model Cadillacs with the license plates "HIS" and "Hers." Smelling money, I went in and asked to see the owner.

A few minutes later, a gentleman in grease stained bib overalls came out to the reception area and introduced himself as the owner. I gave him my card and told him I had been driving back and forth between Lima and Columbus for years but had never seen his building. He said that he and his wife had started their tool and die company in their garage in Bellefontaine and it had grown so rapidly that they had to move into this new building. I said that I had never been in a tool and die plant and asked if he would show me around.

On the factory floor there were approximately 25 tool and die machines. He described the function of each but the only thing that I remembered was they each cost $250,000. Now I really smelled money. After the tour he invited me up to his office, a small platform with a desk overlooking the factory floor. On the desk were a pile of Wall Street Journals. I mentioned that he must be interested in investing and asked who was his broker. He mentioned a small brokerage firm in Columbus and asked me if I knew anything about stocks. He wasn't aware that Merrill Lynch was an investment firm.

I told him a little about myself and Merrill Lynch. He asked me what I thought about Dayton Power and Light, the electric utility serving that part of Ohio. I said that our analyst liked the stock. We chatted a while longer, and I asked if he minded that I stop in from time to time. He said I would be welcome anytime and I left.

The next morning my office phone rang. "Biederman, is that you? This is John T. up to Bellefontaine. Remember me? Do you still like Dayton Power and Light?" I said yes and he said, go ahead and buy me 10,000 shares, 5,000 in my name and 5,000 in my wife's name.

After filling out the new account forms and placing the order, I asked him why he was giving me the order since he already had a broker at the other firm. He said "I've been doing business with them for a number of years but you're the only "stock broker feller" who ever stopped in the plant and asked about my business. Needless to say, asking about someone's success made quite an impression with me.

The other topic that works like a charm is asking about the prospect's interests in life. The beauty of calling on the person at their home or place of business is that the evidence of their interests is usually all around on the desk, walls, bookshelves, etc. Remember Harvey MacKay's advice that the most important reading a salesperson may ever do is the wall of the client's home or office.

Asking a prospect about the story behind a picture, plaque, or trophy is often the best way to utilize the Eureka Factor. Remember Dr. Malandro's words, "people want to be fully understood and are most easily influenced by people they perceive to be like themselves." As they are telling the story behind the picture or other collectible, they get to relive the experience with you and feel subconsciously that you're probably just like them.

On the desk in my office I have four pictures: one of my wife with her favorite horse, Dreamer. She gave me the picture as a Christmas gift and it carries the caption, "Honey, thanks for making my dreams come true.
Love Always, Lois."

The second picture is of our granddaughter, Leah, in an Ohio State University - my alma mater - cheerleader outfit, taken when she was two years old.

The third is of our twin Maltese terriers, Cookie and Daisy, and the fourth, a picture looking over the number eight hole of the Experience at Koele golf course on the island of Lanai in Hawaii.

Ask a question about any of the first three pictures and I'll talk for minutes, telling you exactly why they mean so much to me. Ask about the golf picture and I'll talk even longer, describing how much fun it was to birdie the hole in a PGA pro-am playing with Peter Jacobsen. Golf is my favorite sport and

I've probably shared this story hundreds of times. I still get goose bumps telling it.

As I share my feelings about these pictures that mean so much to me, I'm thinking subconsciously "this person cares about something I love. He or she must be like me." This is the power of the Eureka Factor, a great way to start to build the trust and rapport that clients want with their financial advisor.

By now in the appointment, you've probably established good rapport and it's appropriate to move from personal to business. The client might even prompt you with a comment like, "well I guess you didn't come over just to hear me talk about my grandchildren."

At this point, you should not beat around the bush. It is incumbent upon you to frankly and clearly tell the prospect the reason for your visit and it's important to do so as smoothly as possible. If you stumble for words, you may well damage the favorable impression you've made up to this point. We recommend something like the following:

Prospect: Well I guess you didn't come here today just to hear me talk about my (business, family, pets, hobby, etc)?

Advisor: You're right. I came here to meet you and ask for the opportunity to earn a portion of your investment business.

I undoubtedly used this line hundreds of times in prospecting appointments and I did so because it was something else taught to me by David Stahlberg. David said that anyone who won't give you the "opportunity to earn a portion of their investment business" is probably not worth spending time with and I found that to be true.

In those days, all we had to offer were stocks, bonds, and mutual funds. Today's advisor can provide a whole range of financial services so at this point in the call it's a good time to introduce your value statement; to let the prospect know exactly what you do. They probably think that you're the stereotypical stockbroker who simply buys and sells stocks. To address this impression, we trained our advisors in Southern California to let prospects know that they were not a typical stockbroker. They needed to develop a value statement that indicated their full range of services. One of the most effective of these value statements was the following:

"My team and I provide solutions to successful (niche specialty) for managing their liquid and illiquid assets, arranging asset-based personal or business credit, and protecting against unnecessary income, capital gain, and estate taxation. Are any of these areas of concern to you?"

The typical response of the prospect is often something like "I had no idea you did all of these things. Why don't you tell me a little more? More often than not, however, you will probably hear something like, "I already have a financial advisor, or broker, or manager and at this point, if you decide that you would really like the prospect as a client, you'll have to start "earning their business." We call the process "Responding," the next chapter in SMART©Marketing.

Activities:

1. Practice using the Eureka Factor with people that you meet. Ask them about the story of their success or their strong interests in life and take note of their responses.
2. Practice the transition from personal to business with an associate, spouse, etc until the words literally roll off of your lips.
3. Develop a strong value statement that succinctly and effectively conveys to prospects that you're different from the typical stockbroker.
4. Practice the response to "I already have a broker", or "I'm already taken care of" because you're going to hear these lines time and again in your career.

7
Responding

As we noted earlier, most affluent prospects already have at least one financial advisor and often use two or three. Quite often, they've done business with the person or persons for years and may even have a close personal as well as business relationship, so even though you've met the prospect and, hopefully, made an excellent impression through your use of the Eureka Factor, you're usually going to have to do something outstanding to get them to open an account or transfer their existing account to you.

Fortunately, the typical level of service in our industry has become mediocre at best. In the 1980 and 90's both the equity and bond markets were strong and it was relatively easy to establish and maintain a book of business. Superior client service became a lost art and as a result many clients have become dissatisfied with the way they're treated. In fact, one poll conducted by a major brokerage firm found that only 47% of affluent clients were satisfied and the biggest reason was that they rarely hear from their broker and when they do, it's usually to sell them something.

Ironically, in the 1980's one influential consultant who trained advisors at several large firms told them that it's important to always appear to be very busy and successful to their clients. He advised that the only time you should talk to them is when an order is involved. Isn't it interesting then that now some research indicates that the only time the client hears from their advisor, is when he or she wants to sell them something.

As I mentioned earlier, it will be rare when you open an account or write an order on the first appointment. In fact, you may well be actually rejected by a prospect. But if so, don't give up. In fact there are only three reasons to walk away: (1) they already have an account with your firm, (2) they don't have any money, and (3) they're not someone you want to do business with. If these three disqualifiers are not present, stay in the game because the other firm can drive the client away or you can take the client away with superior business and personal service.

What can the other firm do to drive the client away? They can make a serious operational mistake. They can lose a lot of money with bad investment advice. The other broker can retire, leave the business, be disciplined, or go to another firm which the client doesn't care for.

What can you do to take the client away? In SMART©Marketing, we call it delivering on the four C's: client focus, communication, client wisdom, and caring.

Client Focus: Research indicates that many advisors are market or investment focused. That is, they spend the majority of their time researching investments, following the markets, devising investment strategies, and discussing the market with their peers. On the other hand, client focused advisors spend the majority of their time meeting and talking with client and prospects. It's been shown that client focused advisors open more accounts, raise more assets, do more business, and receive more referrals.

Communication: Many affluent clients prefer to hear from their advisor 20-30 times a year or at least every thirty days. One third of these proactive "touches" should be business related: a buy/sell/or swap recommendation, research on a present holding, information on their own company, industry, or a competitor; a referral to their own business, etc.

Two thirds of the "touches" should be of a personal nature: a birthday or anniversary card, a call just to say hello, a personal favor, a question about something in their life, ie children, vacation, etc. If you are touching the prospect 20-30 times per year and they're hearing from their present broker only once or twice a year, sooner or later, you're going to win.

Client Wisdom: Financial services is a highly commoditized business. A client has access to virtually every product or service from any number of sources, brokers, bankers, insurance agents, etc often at less cost than yours. We maintain that the only thing in our business that cannot be commoditized is the depth of knowledge you have of your clients and prospects. Therefore, you should know almost as much about your top 25 clients and prospects as you know about your best friends, ie personal history, family background (spouse, children, parents, and siblings), business background and future plans, lifestyle (special interests, hobbies, sports, clubs, social life), and religious and political preferences. Information is power and the more business and personal information you possess, the better positioned you are to acquire and retain a client.

Caring: There's an old saying that clients don't care how much you know until they know how much you care. Demonstrate your caring by constantly delivering superior business and personal service. In his book, "Influence, The Psychology of Persuasion," Dr. Robert Cialdini describes five principles of influence, the first being the Rule of Reciprocity. He states that the Rule has applied in every civilization known to mankind; that it's one of the most potent weapons of influence that we have at our disposal, and that a small initial favor can produce a much larger return favor. In many discussions with advisors they've told me that the application of the Rule of Reciprocity has won them very significant clients and amounts of business. Four of my favorites are as follows:

Case study # 17
The $13,000,000 piggy bank – John and his partner had a client who had a much larger account with a competitor and often sang the praises of his other firm. The client and his wife had just completed a $20,000,000 home in a very upscale California community. John told the client that they were going to be in his area over the weekend and asked if they might stop by to see the new home. He agreed and on a Saturday morning they stopped by, were introduced to the man's spouse who was obviously very proud of it and led them on a tour. During the tour they met the couple's five-year old son who wanted them to see his room where he had a beat up old leather piggy bank.

On the way home, they stopped at Discovery Zone and bought a new piggy bank and had it shipped to the young man. The next week the client called them over to his office. The first thing he gave them was a crayoned thank you note from his son and second, was the $13,000,000 account statement from the competitor. He said that his wife had made it clear that he should transfer the account to John and his partner because the competitor had never talked with her, had never visited their home, and certainly had never given their son a piggy bank.

Case study # 18

The $26,000,000 cufflinks: A young advisor with a large national firm in Chicago had been trying to prospect a family in the Midwest that was rumored to be worth well over a billion dollars. For a year, he persisted in calling and writing with no results. After attending our SMART©Marketing program, he Googled the patriarch of the family and found that his passion in life was a small college in his home state. The FA bought a pair of cufflinks with the college crest on their website and had them shipped to the prospect along with his card and a note. Within days, the man called the advisor to thank him for the thoughtful gift, opened an account, and gave him an order to buy $26,000,000 worth of securities.

Case study # 19

The $17,000,000 airplane flight: I received a call from a young advisor who had a prospect who had just sold his business for over $17,000,000. The advisor had established a good relationship with the prospect, but nevertheless was told that the proceeds of the sale were going to be invested with the trust department of his bank because they had treated him well as a business client. The advisor asked me what he could do to earn the business and I asked him what were the man's passions in life. He stated that the man was an avid amateur pilot and that one of his dreams in life was to own a Cessna Citation. I instructed the young man to call the Cessna PR department in Wichita, Kansas, and see if they could send him a Citation poster suitable for framing or a model of the plane. Cessna, to their credit, did something even better. They had their sales representative in the area contact the advisor and invited him and the prospect to take a demo ride on a Citation. Better yet, they even allowed the man to take over the controls during the flight. As they alighted from the demo flight, the man turned to the advisor and said, "you've got my account."

Case study # 20

The last example of the power of the rule happened with me before I even knew of its existence. In 1969, I called the CEO of a publicly held company in

Columbus whom I had met at his club's invitational tennis tournament the previous weekend. I asked him for the opportunity to earn a portion of the company's investment business and was told politely but quite firmly that it wouldn't happen. He said that the family who owned his investment bank also owned his commercial bank and if they found out he was doing business with Merrill Lynch, they might cut off his credit line.

Not to be discouraged, I asked myself what was important in the life of a CEO of a small publicly held company and decided that it might well be the price of his stock. There was no CNBC in those days and stock quotes were only available during the day by calling a NYSE or NASD member firm, so I had my assistant call his secretary just before noon each day and just after the market close with a quote on his company stock.

Three business days later I received a call from the CEO. He asked, "why are you calling with these quotes? I told you that we couldn't give you any business." I said that it was no bother and I just thought that he and his CFO might like to know how the stock was doing. He said they appreciated the information but reiterated that they couldn't give me any business.

Four business days later, he called and said, "we've finally figured out a way to give you some business. We get a lot of people calling who want to buy our stock and don't have a broker. Would you mind if we referred them to you? That summer, a very slow one in the brokerage business, the company sent me 35 clients, one of whom bought 25,000 shares of the stock which resulted in a very substantial commission for yours truly. I didn't know it at the time, but the Rule of Reciprocity was at work for me.

We have many other examples of the use of the rule of reciprocity, so obviously, as Dr. Cialdini states, the Rule has phenomenal power. It's most effective, however, when your gesture addresses something the client or prospect is passionate about. That's where Client Wisdom comes into play. If you know enough about your clients and prospects to understand their passions, you can demonstrate that you care much more effectively than the typical advisor who knows little and you'll find yourself opening more substantial accounts. As you do, to maximize your success, you'll need to leverage these affluent relationships, the next and last step of SMART©Marketing entitled Triggering.

Action Steps:
1. Read Dr. Robert Cialdini's book, "Influence, the Psychology of Persuasion"
2. Whatever CRM system you use, make copious notes about the interests and activities of your clients, prospects, and centers of influence+.

8
Triggering

Earlier in the book we described the production profile of the average financial advisor. We stated that for those who survive the first two years in the business, it takes them five years to get to approximately $300,000 and then they plateau in and around that level for the rest of their career. We feel that there are two main reasons for the plateau effect:

1. They stop prospecting because they don't enjoy doing it. In fact, most regard it as downright painful and most humans seek pleasure and avoid pain.
2. They find their clients one by one instead of leveraging one relationship into many others.

In his great book, "Marketing to the Affluent," which should be required reading for all advisors, Tom Stanley offers an analogy to leveraging relationships. He asks "if you were a submarine commander in WW II and were charged with the task of sinking enemy ships, would you rather find them one by one or in a convoy?" However, Tom states that most otherwise successful sales people never fully leverage their relationships with clients.

In our SMART©Marketing seminars over the past ten years, my partners and I tested Tom's theory and found him to be spot on. We've conducted the following experiment with over 7000 advisors. We ask them to picture the home of their very best client and estimate its value. Depending on the area of the country, the home is usually valued at several million dollars or much more. We then ask them to estimate the value of the home next door and as you would expect, it's priced in the same range. We then ask if it's possible that the next-door neighbor might be a good client and do they have that person as a client. Believe it or not, we've only found three advisors out of the 7,000 who have the neighbor of their best client.

We've discovered several reasons why otherwise successful advisors are not good at leveraging relationships:

1. They don't think about it.

   One very good producer in California had a client who lived in a $30+ million home in Hillsborough, one of the wealthiest suburbs of San Francisco. We took her through the "next door neighbor" exercise and she could not believe that she had never thought about her client's neighbor.

   Another million dollar producer in the Southeast had a paving contractor as his best client who at one time had been the President of his industry's trade association, knew wealthy paving contractors all over the country, and would have been happy to introduce his advisor to them. As usual, however, the advisor had no other paving contractors as clients because, as he told me, he had never thought about it.

2. They've relied on traditional marketing techniques to build their business, ie telephone cold calling, seminars, direct mail, etc. Those techniques usually result in one by one client acquisition and result in a few large clients and many small ones. We call them "Las Vegas marketing" – you roll the dice and take your chances!

3. They've been trained to ask their clients for referrals. Referrals have been held out to be the holy grail of client acquisition by training consultants for years. Unfortunately, referrals are not very effective in leveraging relationships. I know this because at Merrill Lynch in the early 80's, we paid an excellent trainer a lot of money to teach our advisors how to get referrals. Our annual surveys indicated that 91% of clients would give their advisor a referral if asked, however only 9% were ever asked. We felt that getting advisors to ask a greater percentage of their clients for referrals would produce tremendous results. After two years of intensive referral training, the number of clients asked for a referral remained at 9%. In researching the problem with advisors, we found the following:

a. Most advisors won't ask for a referral. They just forget to ask, or are either afraid of being rejected, afraid of appearing to need business, or afraid of offending the client.

b. In a recent client survey, 83% of affluent clients said that they had a negative feeling when asked for a referral. Advisors may instinctively understand this.

c. The typical response to a request for a referral is "let me think about it." Not only do they not think about it for more than few seconds, but in whose hands is your future while they're thinking about it?

If you're really interested in growing your business, you want the ball in your court.

d. Finally, the advisor has no control over the quality of the referral. They're often referred to someone they would rather not work with but take the referral for fear of offending the referrer.

So if cold calling, direct mail, seminars, and referrals aren't effective in leveraging relationships, what will work. In SMART©Marketing we teach advisors how to find convoys of affluent prospects by leveraging their best relationships. We emphasize three techniques for doing so:

1. Niche specialization
2. The Advice Process
3. Magnetic Marketing

Since we covered niche specialization and the advice process in depth in chapters four and five, let's move directly into magnetic marketing. It's based on the theory that successful people attract other successful people to themselves, just like a magnet and we developed a wheel that looks something like a pinwheel (pictured below.) The president of one regional brokerage firm calls it the "Wheel of Fortune" because it's so powerful in reminding advisors of the tremendous value of constantly thinking about leveraging their relationships with clients, prospects, and centers of influence.

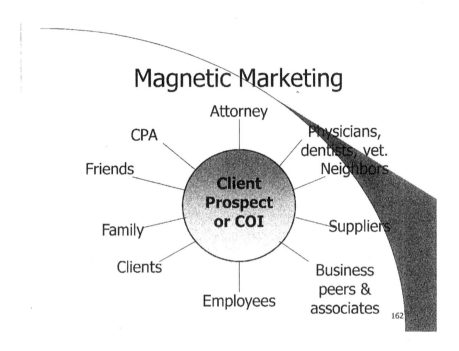

As with the advice process, I was lucky enough to stumble on the concept of Magnetic Marketing when I was a Merrill Lynch producer in Columbus, Ohio. It allowed me to turn one wealthy prospect into over twenty very prosperous clients. The story goes as follows: one day in my home town, Lima, Ohio, I decided to call on the owner of the largest department store in town, Mr. G. After some small talk, I asked him for the opportunity to earn a portion of his investment business. Surprisingly, he stated that he didn't have any because he was too busy with the store to have time to invest. He said, "you should be talking with Mabel (his wife), she handles all of our investments."

My next question was straight from the advice process: "what would be the best way to reach her?" He called her and said, "I've got this young fellow here from Merrill Lynch and I'm sending him out to the house to meet you."

A few minutes later I was at their beautiful home talking with Mrs. G who said that investing was one of her hobbies and that she had made a lot of money in the market, especially in one company, Simplicity Pattern. I asked her how she decided on that stock and she told me that her other hobby was sewing. She liked their patterns, bought a few hundred shares of the stock, and several years later had a profit of over $500,000. She added that not only did she own the stock but all of the members of her sewing bee did so also.

Sensing an opportunity, I asked if she thought the members would like to know what Merrill Lynch thought about Simplicity Pattern and asked if I might attend their next meeting, hand out our latest research report, and conduct a brief seminar on the company. She thought that was a wonderful idea and a week later, I was speaking to nine of the wealthiest women in Lima, Ohio. I started with one prospect and now had nine.

I thought this can be a goldmine. "I wonder who else Mr. G knows that I should meet." Lima was a city of 50,000 and Mr. G was one of its wealthiest citizens. I assumed that he would know the wealthiest man in town who was a business legend in Ohio and the second wealthiest person in the state. The day I spoke to the sewing bee, I stopped by Mr. G's store and asked him if knew Mr. JG. He said, "Johnny, I've known him all my life. He's one of my best friends."

Again, from the advice script I asked if he thought I should be calling on Mr. JG. He answered "he's got more money than God and he loves the stock market. One of his best friends founded Litton and Teledyne. I can't imagine how much of those two stocks he owns."

I asked, what would be the best way to reach him and again, he picked up the phone, called Mr. JG, and said, "Johnny, I've got a young man here from Merrill Lynch who would like to meet you. When can you see him?" He put down the phone and said, "go see him early tomorrow morning."

I called my office manager in Columbus and said, "Lee, I have an appointment with God tomorrow. I'm scared to death. Will you make the call with me?"

That afternoon I drove the ninety miles back to Columbus and the next morning we left for Lima at 5:30AM to be sitting on the steps of Mr. JG's company when he drove up. His first words to us were "where did you boys stay last night, the Holiday Inn?" I told him we had been in Columbus and drove up that morning to see him. He said, "you must have left there around 5AM. Anyone who gets up that early to see me, I want to talk to. Come on in."

We spent over an hour with Mr. JG that morning. He told us that his broker was a senior partner of one of the most highly respected investment banking firms in Ohio. He also told us everything he owned, including over ten thousand shares each of Litton and Teledyne, both of which were selling then around $150. He also invited us to feel free to stop in whenever we were in Lima. How long do you think it would have taken to meet Mr. JG by cold calling?

Back in our office, I read Merrill Lynch's research on Teledyne and Litton and found that our analyst loved the former, but thought Litton should be sold. Calling Mr. JG immediately, I told him about the opinion and asked if he would like to talk with the analyst. The next day my manager and I drove back to Lima and had a conference call with her in Mr. JG's office. Afterwards, he said "Very interesting, let me think about it."

Two weeks later, he called me and sold 5,000 shares of Litton, some for himself, some for his son, Bob, some for his son-in-law, Jack, and some for his daughter, who happened to be married to the second wealthiest man in Lima. By this time, I had Mrs. G as a client, four of the eight other women in her sewing bee, and four members of the JG family – all from the magnetic marketing process.

The next step was to figure out who Mr. JG knew that I wanted as a client. I had been trying unsuccessfully to call on the trust officer at the largest bank in town. He wouldn't talk to me because I was a retail, not an institutional broker. It was common knowledge that Mr. JG was the largest shareholder of the bank, I asked him if I should be calling on the bank. He told me that they had a large trust department and I could probably do a lot of business there. I mentioned that the trust officer wouldn't see me and he said, "would you like to meet the president of the bank? Why don't you come to the Breakfast Club meeting with me on Saturday morning."

I had grown up in Lima but had never heard of the Breakfast Club. It consisted of six of the wealthiest, most influential men in Northwestern Ohio, including the president of the bank, and Mr. JG was its leader. He took me to the meeting and introduced me to the group as "his broker at Merrill Lynch." It was a fascinating experience as I heard them discuss how they planned to corner the cable TV market in northwestern Ohio, which they did, and who they were going to elect as the next senator from Ohio, which they did also.

After the introduction from Mr. JG, I had no trouble the next week seeing the trust officer of the bank. I opened an account with the bank and over the next two years, did business with all but one of the members of the breakfast club.

The business with this group alone allowed me to exceed the $100,000 commission level in my first full year in the business. In those days, $100,000 was the recognized level of success in our industry.

By the way, don't be surprised that it was relatively easy to get personal introductions to so many successful people. This is the way the world works. All of your best clients and prospects have a magnetic field around them. Your job is to get inside that field and leverage the relationships. I am convinced that the Magnetic Marketing concept was the principal reason our rookies in Southern California District were so much more successful than their peers at Merrill Lynch.

In fact, we had one young man, Mr. C, who was the most successful rookie with whom I had the pleasure to work in thirty years. I won't mention his first name because he is so well known in his area, but I think you will instantly identify with his level of success: $250,000 in his first twelve months, $756,000 in the second twelve, and nearly $1,000,000 in the third twelve. He became so well known in Merrill Lynch that I began getting calls from my peers around the firm asking me if he was for real. Did he come from a big money background? Did he luck into a huge client? Was he churning accounts?
When I told them that he was a twenty-six year old Korean- American, had joined us from a pharmaceutical company, was new to Southern California,

and had built his business entirely on his own, they asked if we would let him come speak to their advisors. That year, Mr. C spoke to groups in New York City, Washington, D.C., Chicago, San Francisco, and Dallas. He was always asked him how he could possibly do so much business and he humbly told them that whenever he ran out of prospects, he would take out the Magnetic Marketing wheel, ask himself who his best clients knew, and then set about getting introductions from them to new prospects. There's no reason you can't do the same.

Action Steps
1. Complete the "wheel of fortune" on each of your best clients, prospects, or centers of influence.
2. Meet face to face with each of them and ask:
   - Do you know Mr. or Mrs. _____?
   - Should I be calling on them?
   - If you were me, what would be the best way to reach them?
3. If you don't know or can't pre-identify who is in their magnetic field, you can ask, Mr. or Mrs. _____, who is the most successful investor you know? Rest assured that every affluent person knows others. In my Lima example, if I had not correctly assumed that Mr. G knew Mr. JG, I could have asked him who was the most successful investor he knew and would have ended up with the same result, Mr. JG.
4. Master the Advice script, if you have not done so already. It will allow you to get the information you need to know from the "Wheel of Fortune."

9
Summary

We stated in chapter three that to be hugely successful in the investment business, you need to be good at five activities:

1. Identifying affluent prospects
2. Meeting them face to face
3. Building rapport with them
4. Earning all or some of their investment business
5. Leveraging your best relationships into personal introductions to others just like them

Unfortunately, many advisors do not have a coach to help them succeed. In the case of SMART©Marketing, it's possible to be your own coach. I recommend that on a weekly basis you ask yourself five questions:

1. Selecting: Am I successfully penetrating three distinct niches? If not, why not?
2. Marketing: Whatever marketing methods I'm using, are they getting me face to face with several new qualified prospects per week? If not, I should change my marketing approach.
3. Affiliating: Am I building rapport (trust and affection) in these meetings? The evidence of rapport is business and personal information. If I'm obtaining very little information, I need to work of my affiliation skills.
4. Responding: Am I providing superior business and personal service to my qualified prospects via the four C's and the Rule of Reciprocity?
5. Triggering: Am I leveraging my best client, prospect, and center of influence relationships into more qualified people like them?

If you can honestly answer these five questions in the affirmative on a weekly basis, you're well on your way to becoming a SMART©Marketing professional and a very successful financial advisor and I guarantee that you'll make as much money as you would like and have an enormous amount of fun doing it. I wouldn't trade my career for any other and I wish you the same amount of wealth and enjoyment in yours.

Good luck!